MW01096792

"Izzy Wass‹
holds barre
She ranges

She narrates and lyricizes the urban landscape, peopling it with preachers and panhandlers. This is a skilled writer who will lure you into her world. You will not be able to forget it."

~Denise Low, 2007-09 Kansas Poet Laureate,
author of *Shadow Light*

"*When Creation Falls* is an archeological excursion into origins of knowledge and doubt, homecoming and expulsion, real monsters and fictional faiths, and the soul of place and time. Izzy Wasserstein is a time traveler of a poet, from her 'Report to William Stafford' about the immortal and amoral wind, to her confluence of Columbus's landing and biblical Isaac in '1492.' She writes with great verve and vision, continually unearthing memory and history to show the layers of loss bleeding through the present, reminding us that 'we drag our world with us, even to the depths.' Yet this remarkable collection also sees deeply into the wild soul of what's possible, illuminating how 'Tall grass tells the wind's story.' *When Creation Falls*, calls on us to live our truths, even if we come up short, reminding us, 'The hammer is as heavy as it needs to be./ It was made for you./ Strike again.' I love these poems and found myself dazzled on every page by Wasserstein's clear intelligence, hard-won wisdom, and brave music."

~Caryn Mirriam-Goldberg,
2009-13 Kansas Poet Laureate,
and author of *Everyday Magic: Fieldnotes
on the Mundane and Miraculous*

"In *When Creation Falls*, Izzy Wasserstein guides us through her Topeka upbringing, the blink of millions of years, tornado sirens, and the sermons that don't always deliver. She gives powerful voice to the golem, her past namesake, poverty's ghosts, the time traveler, the bends in lonely creeks, metaphorical riffs on cancer, and bison skulls. These inspiring poems are personal, political, and persistent in reminding us that even in confronting our fears of falling short, we are always writing to discover the lasting warmth of love, to find what lies in the footnotes, and to 'reject the sin of silence.'"

~Juan J. Morales,
author of *The Siren World* &
*The Handyman's Guide to End Times*

"Izzy Wasserstein is broadly and deeply learned, but also committed to the clear utterance. The poems in *When Creation Falls* are as transparent as glass—not a window, but a corrective lens, restoring detail and dignity to world of distortions and cynical simplifications. This is a poet furious at injustice but suspicious of fury. I kept thinking, as I read, of Auden's 'September 1, 1939'—'All I have is a voice/ To undo the folded lie' —and it was satisfying to discover that poem's last line in one of this book's last poems: 'Show an affirming flame.' Auden, of course, infamously renounced the poem, and Wasserstein acknowledges that fraught history in order to craft a durable new affirmation for herself: 'And if my words/ become ugly, if I recant/ every last kind thought,/ if the lines of my face/ twist in cruelty,/ may these soundings/ outlast me.' In a poem addressed 'To the Child I Will Never Have,' her final piece of advice is 'Make something beautiful.' Someone must have told her the same thing.

~Eric McHenry, 2015-17 Kansas Poet Laureate

# When Creation Falls
Poems by Izzy Wasserstein

Meadowlark (an imprint of Chasing Tigers Press)
meadowlark-books.com
P.O. Box 333, Emporia, KS 66801

ISBN: 978-0-9966801-9-6

Library of Congress Control Number: 2018936428

# When Creation Falls

## Poems by Izzy Wasserstein

**A MEADOWLARK BOOK**

# Contents

III: *Apocalypse*

*for my parents*

For we wrestle not against flesh and blood, but against principalities, against powers, against the rulers of the darkness of this world, against spiritual wickedness in high *places*.

–Ephesians 6:12

# 1: Paleontology

## Where I'm From

I'm from cottonwood allergies,
from late night Royals baseball
on AM radio, from the trailer
where my grandparents,
then my parents, lived,
from tornado sirens
and peanut butter and honey,
from gravel roads
and Bible study,
from Wisdom Booklets
and Creation Research seminars,
from homeschooling,
from menorahs,
from Wildcat country
and Fred Phelps, from
Encyclopedia Brown
and Charles Dickens,
from John Brown,
from the puckered scar the bat carved over my eye,
from poison ivy and creek beds,
from stray cats and snapping turtles,
from my infant brother's grave,
from Gatekeeper Hobbies.

I'm from prairies, and mesas,
and prairies again. I'm from books
read aloud, from C. S. Lewis,
from Phil Levine and Leslie Marmon Silko,
from Star Wars and Star Wars,
from Reagan,
from the Cross to the sky,
from the sky to the opened sky,
from gods to beauty.

I'm from wild blackberries,
from hymns, from milky way nights,
from the clatter, the hammer of rain
on tin roofs.

## Married Student Housing

I do not remember
the layout of that apartment,
nor the cockroaches
my parents tell me were everywhere,
fleeing from the light,
crunching under our feet in the dark.
I remember the Iranian neighbors'
kind smiles. My mother's words,
*They fled the Shah,*
as incomprehensible as my father's textbooks
and their strange symbols.

I remember the big oak tree in the quad. (Was it big?
Was it an oak? That is how I
remember it.) My trike on the uneven sidewalks.
I do not remember other children.

*You were so lonely,* my mother says.
I suppose it is true.
I dipped my toy fishing pole
into a mud puddle, asking the teenagers
who came by if they wanted to fish with me.

I imagine they broke it with careless malice,
the way teens do, especially when they live
in married student housing, especially
when Kansas curls around them like a curse.
I brought the rod inside,
snapped in half. I recall no sorrow, only
the look in my mother's eyes, heavy with the knowledge
she must have understood
was already growing in me.

## Services

Six years old, I sit in the second row
at Bible Church. I sing enthusiastically,
off-key: *when the roll is called up yonder*.

I know rolls of paper towels, rolling
up paper into a scepter or horn.
No one has ever taken roll for me
or told me where they will take it.
I think of hay bales coiled.

I do not speak. In church,
children may sing, but are not to ask questions.
The pastor, the elders,
the men may pray aloud (this means
they speak, not that they shout). Children,
women, are to be silent.

They are to serve
and be cherished. Women are a complement
to their husbands, to be a helpmeet.
(I know *help* and *meet*.)

There is the band that leads worship (war
ship), and the banned: sec-u-lar music,
anything with witches, language,
heathens, inter-course.

The pastor says *We know God exists*
*because we are his creatures. We know*
*God when we accept* (except?) *him into our hearts.*
A man knows his wife,
but this means something else.

*We know*, the pastor says. No doubt. No, doubt
is wrong. Thomas staring at the holes
in His hands. We are cut off, severed. He
makes us whole. To doubt is to sin.
Even in our hearts, we are not allowed
to sin. To doubt aloud is to blaspheme.

The sermon ends. We bow our heads,
go out into the world, into our damned nation.

## Girl from the Great Plains at a Denver Funeral

In the windless cemetery, in the mountain's shadow,
dirt falls on the casket, and this
reminds the girl of the first hint of rain.
She is eight, and never knew
the woman they bury. But she has seen
the mourners step forward, hesitant.
They follow her grandfather who, queued, stooped,
taps his cane, as if passing
through a servant's door.
The girl hesitates, then joins the line, stands over the hole,
the glossed redwood spread with dirt.
She grips the shovel. The thud of earth
is louder here.
Her grandfather stands, the cane forgotten.

Once, the girl visited the beach,
and carried a pebble home, cool and smooth as an egg
in her pocket. She tells herself
this too she must carry. She grasps
a handful of dust, lets it slide between her fingers.

Later, there is food, hushed laughter,
stories: the meals the dead woman would set out
for Sabbath, great piles of meat,
and mutter how her children grew fat;
her refusal to euphemize;
her contempt for the fool rabbi
who long ago eulogized her husband
as though he were a devout man.

The next morning, the long drive home.
The mountaintop is rosy with dawn.
*Thank you*, the girl's grandfather says, *for helping me
bury my mother*. The girl rubs her hands together,
straightens her back. Prairie opens before them.
Tall grass tells the wind's story.

## Family Photo

My father stands to one side, dwarfed
by three of us, bald head, broad smile.
A step ahead and to his right, my mother,
plain blouse and long dark hair.
I stand, the oldest, off-balance, matted
hair and cokebottle glasses. Matthew
is in full beard, half grin, bright red sweater.
Rachel's hair is dark as mine, but straight
as her posture, unreadable expression in her
black eyes. Grace, straw-haired, with open
smile and tensed shoulders. Beth, the dancer,
seems poised on the lip of action, ready to burst
from the frame. Joel, unmistakably Matthew's
brother, including the mischief in his eyes.
Rose is a spring wound tightly, her glance askew,
looking to something we can't quite see.

Not pictured: David, a decade dead.
Johnathon and Jessica, who we don't yet know,
in their orbits
between foster homes, elliptical paths
even now drawing their faces in and out of focus.

# Reconstruction

*I*

Later, I tried to reconstruct the moment:
your ever-present smile, small and crooked,
like you knew something the rest of us
missed, the book in your hand.
Part of a series whose name was gone
before you were. Your hair, perpetually ragged.
Did your shoulders slump, did some whisper
move in the privacy of your eyes? I could never recall.
Now even your face recedes.

*II*

At the zoo, clowning, you turned to the hippos,
loudly proclaimed: *Look at the underwater elephants*
in a child's voice. A stranger frowned, shook his head.
We laughed. Later, we scrawled the phrase
across the camp's memory wall, our ridiculous memento
of a summer spent going nowhere, tumbling there
like stones down a slick hill. Now new campers'
words are scrawled, palimpsest, in its place.

*III*

With such small treacheries the past is stolen.
Even the exhaust, filling your car, dissipated
quickly once they opened the door, its only evidence
written across your body.

## At the Bend in Cow Creek

Leaves slide across the dark surface;
brown water divides prairie.
The swimming hole is far removed from human sounds—
only wind through trees, a woodpecker downstream.

You leap, as always, head first. Below, discarded
trash, rusted beyond recognition,
catches the top of your head. Weeks later, you'll
regain some movement in your fingers.

We draw you out, wait for civilization
to claim you, paramedics traveling fifteen miles
from Hutchinson. Long enough to know:
we drag our world with us, even to the depths.

# Night Shift at the Computer Lab

The last students left hours
ago, summer stragglers who hope
Myspace and message boards
will distract from whatever's waiting
at home. But even they are eventually chased
into the night by the buzz of monitors
and fluorescents, out into the streetlight
and oak leaves along 17th Street,
until you're here alone.
Midnight's an hour away
and you've fixed the printer,
sent reports, waited at the helpdesk
to answer questions no one's asking,
surfed the web, read some book incapable
of holding your attention, and you start
to dream of real work, any work, even
days spent washing dishes,
tearing down buildings, burning
fields, even your buddy's job,
watching the unused gate
to a construction site, guarding
it with a walkie-talkie and silence.
If the security guard didn't stroll through

every ninety minutes, you might
believe you were the last one on campus,
keeping those desktops open
for students who weren't coming,
who were off drinking or studying
or driving aimlessly down Wanamaker,
looking for something to shake them awake.
It's as if the Rapture has come
or the last stars have burned out,
and you check your watch. 11:17.
Forty-three minutes until you reboot
the servers, one by one, send another report,
and wander home over rain-slick streets.

# I Rarely Write Before Dawn

> I get pen and paper, take a glance out of the window
> (often it is dark out there), and wait.
> —William Stafford

I wake to see the streetlights
pulled apart by fog. The air falls like a rough blanket
over my shoulders. Soon the buses will shudder
on their way to schools, and the dogs
will chase each other through the backyard. I stand
on the porch and listen to the train, a fog-horn
moving through the night, crying *danger*.
We have been at war though my adult life,
though they call wars *military actions* these days.
I tell my students there was a time, not long ago,
where we thought we'd all go up in atomic ash,
leaving a withered world and the flash outlines of bodies.

A distant bell marks the hour,
and I think of the sailor saying *there are no fish left*,
and whether the school children's children
will find coral as otherworldly as the Tasmanian tiger.
The fog distorts sound, makes dark mourners
of the trees. Rain comes in the afternoon.

## Touring Topeka, Kansas

The Frito-Lay plant hunches over Topeka Boulevard
like a great cat tensed,
or some days pulls itself compact before the gray
prairie sky. (To see it breathe

is to accept personification.) Today it disgorges smoke,
industrial stench that burrows in your clothes.
Mud and snow blend across the Boulevard.
Private trucks, contractors, plow the streets
or leave them buried.

The capitol dome shakes open the sky
as men like bees scale its scaffolds. At the crest,
the bronze Indian eternally readies his bow.
Union workers chant slogans—

the State proclaims itself *right-to-work*.
Two blocks from here the bodies
of immigrants amongst the squalor.
Their boss confiscated their green cards.

The city tore down the old mental hospital,
hauled away asbestos and window bars.
Gravestones remain, in flat white rows
overlooking the Kansas River,

where ice cuts wounds across water.
An easy walk from there to Westboro.
The church proclaims GOD HATES FAGS
and flies an inverted American Flag
over an eight-foot fence.

The parishioners pace busy sidewalks
with neon signs proclaiming THANK GOD
FOR DEAD SOLDIERS and AMERICA
IS DOOMED (four-year-olds holding signs
and Reverend Fred Phelps

searching for his next lawsuit). And here, look, the pine
we planted in memory of my brother, in the backyard
of our old house. No plaque adorns it.
Through the chain-link in the corner of the yard, it grows.

## Confessions of a Homeschooler

Don't confess it at all, if you can help it,
though it is no secret. It's better to conceal
a long scar, puckered and pink,
or the form of a long-dead twin
knotted to your side. This isn't shame,
only the desire not to be an exhibit.
No matter how stiffly you hold yourself,
no matter how proud your bearing,
you're the one behind glass, and their eyes
always go wide. It is better to pass,
to elide the strange gaps in your knowledge—
biology, poetry, television. Push through them
like ellipses. Other chasms won't be concealed:
a decade's pop culture escaped, the staccato
beats of hesitation in large groups, that ache
carried that is not quite
what other children call loneliness.
Even true answers must claw their way up your throat:

*No, I've never won a spelling bee.*
*No trouble getting into college.*
*No, it wasn't so bad.*
*No, I wouldn't recommend it.*

Harder is what they don't ask,
the evaluating look, the puzzle.
They are deciding
whether you are strange enough
that they should have known.

## The New House

In the basement, twice the size
of our old trailer, I heard phantom footsteps upstairs,
not my father at work, nor my mother
and siblings nearby, leaning over textbooks.

Before, I could hear the front door open
from anywhere in the trailer, even my favorite spot
at the desk in my parents' bedroom,
the only place overlooking
not the steep gravel hill and the wind-torn trailers,
but a sweep of dirt and high grass
all the way to the highway.
When Dad told us to pack
I did not know I would never again hear
storms on the metal roof, except in my sleep,
the sound that even today is rain-song for me.

I did not know we had been poor,
nor the silence of suburban nights.
I did not know I would never again live
near children my own age. I did not know
what it meant for a house to settle.

I only knew there were *things*
upstairs, monsters I had not imagined.
I never told anyone what I heard.
I pressed my back to the basement wall
and listened.

## Memory (Fragments)

after Raza Ali Hasan

*I*
Cries of pain drew me to the backyard,
where the dogs had cornered a stray cat.

By the time I chased them off, her rib-bare
frame was shuddering, panic stricken.

She died quickly, bone-thin, matte-black fur in patches.
Had she sought the mercy of the tooth's edge?

*II*
She wore Alzheimer's like a rotten cloak,
wandering neighborhoods where once

she'd seen wheat rolling down to the Kansas River.
Clouded eyes stared uncomprehending. She played

old hymns beautifully. In the afterlife, what memory
will she carry? Days of rocking in her own waste?

*III*
My brother was born imperfectly formed.
Miracle machinery kept him alive for days.

The funeral was lovely, the trees attending
in their austerity, the winter sky

closed and shuttered. I'm told he is in paradise
awaiting us. What man's face will greet me?

## Fracture

The dogs have found a nest

    in the backyard. Infants.

Rabbits? Hard to see.
  half-blind     squeaking white flesh.

    My grandfather scrawls
indecipherable
  across the page.

The machines    punctuate  rhythm
  no one will ever dance to.

*Will*    *Read*
    *Will*
we think he writes.

Pull. Pull it.    Silence. Silence that
    unsteady hand
daemonic rhythm.

Reject it.  Borne    away.

Quick like a dog's   smile/
        swallow.


My grandmother   wandering
    the house
        Alzheimer's
checking for      what?
    locks unbolted.


Some other place.    Borne away.


        Pages torn by some
unsteady      hand
when she plays         piano
    notes rise    shaken beautifully
        awake.        Awake.


Swallowed.       gone.


The doors. Locked.
        Combinations lost.


Born pale
    squealing.

# Aubade

Those days I rose in the darkness, left you sleeping,
with nowhere to go but the call center,
to spend the day troubleshooting Blackberries
and routers, arriving before the sun slides
over the Sandias, and leaving in the cold
February night. It happened imperceptibly.
One night I was sleeping over. Before long,
my dog was staying with yours.
Days, I listened to the quiet buzz of conversation,
paced back and forth, my arc anchored
by my headset. Evenings I'd pick up takeout,
we'd watch something funny or frightening, anything
to help me forget I will rise, Sunday morning,
for that same commute. A few more months
of call quality checks and hard resets
would have killed me.
But one night I came home and found you
wearing my sweater. *It keeps me warm*, you said,
*I like it for the smell of you*. This is no sentimentality:
know that you kept me orbiting,
those dark months, you gave me your body heat,
something to keep me from driving on,
past the city's sprawl, into the high desert,
into the morning's glare.

## Baseball

A love carved across my face,
a scar above my left eye
where the bat split skin from bone.
A clean blow, nothing like the jagged map
the nurse's needle made in closing it.
I was the only kid at the Topeka Public Library
asking for books about the Black Sox Scandal,
begging the other kids to grab bats
when they preferred football.
Like the oversize glasses I wore,
I'd been lifted from another era.
My family didn't own a television,
so I'd lay awake at night listening
to Fred and Denny call games
on the radio. In the dark, I could smell
the wet grass, chalk and dust,
see the pitcher framed by floodlights.
I loved baseball as I rarely loved anything else,
loved baseball even when it did not love me back.

After the impact, my friends stood over me,
their summer-dark faces blanched.
That night I dreamed I was stepping to the plate.

# Lately I've Been Thinking of Sacrifice

and the charnel-stench of those animals
sold to slaughter in Yaweh's temple,
a curtain of flies outside the Holy of Holies.
What did the people think of such death,
the blood clotting in pools? Were they
terrified of the depth of their sin,
or did the smell of burnt fat and split intestines
grow old as that damp scent in my garage?
And surely the animals, those flawless creatures
chosen, they must not have been so keen on sacrificial
atonement—though scholarship on pigeon theology
is woefully underdeveloped. And death
is easy, I have it on authority—perhaps a slipping off
into a silent sea, or returning to life like a man waking
from too long a slumber: *what time is it?* as he stumbles
into the daylight.

> Give me the costs one must live with.
Moses, silent in the desert, outside the land he was promised;
Cain walking the earth, an unkillable terror;
or Odin, plucking his eye for wisdom,
suffering nine nights to bring his people the written word,
or—as I once heard the story—buggered by a dwarf
to learn magic. And he came home to listen to his son tell him

he was unmanly: not for the fucking,
but for mastering a woman's art. You spend your days
preventing Ragnarök, and that's the thanks you get.
Take Bruce Banner, that god of science
and rage. There's always some pressing disaster,
some need to break the chains from the beast,
turn the world red. And the next morning
you've shredded another shirt, maybe destroyed a town
or hurled a supervillain into orbit. Hulk is gone,
and you have no choice but to walk on, dragging
that weight behind.

## Paleontology

*These tracks are dinosaurs'—*
our guide, white teeth, a ten gallon hat
and new boots—*and these are human.*
*Note the toes.* Peeking between the adults'
legs, I see two sets of prints,
one inside the other, and four—I squint—
no, five digits.

*Four thousand two hundred ninety two*
*years ago, give or take,*
*the dinosaurs fled through*
*the riverbed, as Noah's flood drowned*
*everything behind them. Humans, fleeing*
*God's wrath, ran with the dinosaurs.* His face
is smooth as a child's, his hair salted.

I gawk at the prints. The great lizards
were here once, and I need to believe.
I tell every adult who will listen
someday I will be a paleontologist,
will discover new dinosaurs. I imagine
great Triceratops battling Tyrannosaurs,
Apatosaurus cries heard by missionaries
deep in African jungles.

In groups at the walls of the Texas riverbed,
we cautiously chip away, dust, examine
flaking rocks hoping for fossils,
some ancient—perhaps six thousand years.
Sweat curls into my eyes.
The sky is wide, pale, featureless.

After lunch we gather in the tent.
The preacher reads to us: Genesis,
Job, Revelation. We are in the last days,
our gnostic truth recorded on gold leaf
and ancient stone, if the World
would open their ears. The crowd cries
*Amen*, prays for this wicked generation.

Knowing the beginning, we know
the end. At dusk, I stalk through the canyon:
the earth is alive with the roars of monsters.

# 11: Eschatology

## 85% of Methamphetamine Users Do Not Become Addicts

according to one study.
If every member of my composition class tried it,
perhaps three or four would be hooked. Good
odds or bad? Depends on the upside, I suppose. My students
like to debate the drinking age, 18 and chafing at illogic,
at the slow gravity of their lives,
or back from Afghanistan and writing about what it means
to grow up in a combat zone. What can they
tell the soft teacher with the scar over one eye, professor
at this suburban public school? What image
can they evoke to make her see?

                                                Their fellow students,
the ones who haven't already spun the meth wheel,
have driven down country roads in shaking pickups,
bottles of whiskey pressed between their knees, clattering
across railroad crossings and wheat fields, the sliver of moon
muting gold to gray. In every class someone has a story
about a life destroyed by drunks behind the wheel,
but the numbers don't change: 3 in 10 will know
the twist of metal and plastic, alcohol and impact.

What's acceptable risk for forgetting you live in a dying town
and are no closer to getting out than you were two years ago?

I'm not one for drugs, only alcohol
has ever done anything for me. My brother
would rather listen to voices in his head
than whatever his prescriptions say.
The voices tell him he'll be a movie star, or MMA warrior,
or Batman. Some nights he disappears into the darkness.
I once dreamed of winning the Yale Younger Poets prize.
Try not to judge.

                      I'll admit I'd prefer they avoid meth,
these students, most slumped over their desks at 8 AM,
a couple avid, alert.
I won't guess if their eagerness is enhanced.
15%: Those aren't odds I'd want a loved one to gamble on,
not worth the high, I'd say, not worth clashing with the law
who'd like nothing more than to grin at the camera, assault rifles
in hand, over bags of cash and Crystal.
No math but my own.

                      My students don't understand
how the experts they read, debating the drinking age,
can all share facts, yet disagree. One young woman,
lines already forming in the hollows beneath her eyes,
asks me to explain. She's writing
about her foster brother's addict mom.
I want to tell her, *don't believe people who tell*
*you how to be happy*. Tell them all, *they don't know how*
*any more than you do*. I shrug.
*These are just numbers*, I say. *You have to give them meaning*.
It's Friday, and the weekend stretches before them like dark
   train tracks.
Where we're from, no crossing is regulated.

## Men with Bison Skulls

Photograph, 1870s

One man stands atop the pile,
holds a single skull,
as if to make the sight comprehensible:
the mound take shape,
white faces, eyeless stares, stacked
forty feet high, thrice
as wide. By then Kansas
was littered with sun-bright bones
abandoned by hunters who cared
only for hides or sport.
The government encouraged
slaughter: as herds disappeared
tribes would accept Reservations.
Soon those silent skeletons
were in demand: for china,
fertilizer, sugar.
Settlers gathered ribs, femurs,
sterna, sold them for $8 a ton.
Men were paid to stack,
prepare them for grinding.
Their boss, bottom of the frame,
pristine in top-hat
and coat, leans against
the wall of bone, dwarfed by it.
His face is a blur, his eyes
swallowed by the years.

## *Tiktaalik Roeae*

I.   Ellesmere Island, 2004

Four years we scraped and chipped
in riverbeds, Devonian,
swept between the glaciers
and aurora borealis.
They must have lived in places
like this, fish with fins like legs,
ancestors to tetrapods,
lizards, birds, mammals.
One day the flat head edges
from streambed.
Inuit elders suggest
its name. *Tiktaalik*: freshwater fish.
Listen: do not say *ancient*.
You underestimate.
If your life was one second,
she lived fifty seven days ago.

II.        Laurentia, 275 MA

She made her home on the stream's edge
sliding through shallows,
searching for prey, her low head twisting,
seeking the next meal.
With food scarce, she pushed herself
to dry land, foraging across tropic banks,
fins edging across the surface.
Where her ancestors kept to the streams
she finds resources on land as well.
She grows. Mates. Passes on her genes.

III.    Topeka, Kansas, 2014

The temptation, anthropocentric: the fish crawled
shores, our ancestor. As though evolution
an architect, crafting to a blueprint.
No. Nothing urged ancient fish
to these beds but the oldest impulses: Survive. Reproduce.
No teleology, no end goal: just desire. The gene
copies itself, mutates, life branches,
paths unfold and die. The most common
reaction to change: extinction.
And, amidst those billions upon billions
of selections, we dream some God
or Fate brought us here. And then,
our breath caught:
fin's curve in exposed bone.

## Eureka

We dream revelations like avalanche:
one moment silence, and the next
a roar and cascade
until we are buried by insight,
as Archimedes, leaping from his bath,
shouted his naked triumph.
What's revealed may crack
us open in an instant,
an oak shorn by a strong wind.
We do not see the subtle building
of currents into a storm,
beginnings made clear only in endings.

So Darwin works his careful way,
noting, labeling, observing:
the patient naturalist cast his eye
upon mockingbird, finch,
tortoise, until the weight
of variations pressed
and overflowed, and, ponderously,
the great man began to write.

And even then, as evidence spilled
around him, Wallace found
the same vista, emerging through
data, the eye pulling back, bringing

to focus the mechanism,
the answer for both to see:
elegant brutality of their origins.

## A Time Traveler Sends a Postcard Home

I found this card in ruins,
a tourist trap above a volcano.
The air reeks of sulfur, but the view—
storm-gray rocks and lava trails
to violent sea—magnificent desolation.
What year this is, I cannot say,
those readouts have burned out long ago.
Once I charted the eons
by light pollution or the ice caps
but now I am content to leap
like a child who trusts her father will catch her.
When will this find you? The day of your birth?
Double feature at the drive in? The night we watched
bombs shed the night's skin? The fall
day when rain finally stopped and you said
*this is no way to live*? You were right,
or will be. Rocks melt in the silence.
The water's edge tints red.
An algal bloom,
or some chemical morass.
I will investigate.

    Yours Always,

## To the Mantis Shrimp

The gulf between us is greater
than that between my beige desert home
and the hostile sweeps of coral,
between this keyboard and the crushing
dart of your claws.

Flatter me that the widest gap
is this proud language, this conceit
of speaking to an idea
across the sea's distorting echoes,
as though, if I reached for you,
you would not split my thumb.

I can say (understanding
without wisdom)
that your eyes perceive
far into ultraviolet, wavelengths
forever denied my few cones.
Against this monolith of incomprehension,
I ask what thrill you know, what neurons
fire at the sight of a female's fluoresce,

or alert you to transparent prey
(transparent only to me).
I can no more imagine this
than a fifth dimension,

time's arrow reversed, what strings,
vibrating, give shape to the universe,
what other planes may exist,
strange-hued bubbles rising from the foam
of the multiverse.

Through what small windows we view,
the few degrees of your vision, the few colors
of mine, who says *beige*, and trusts,
with a poet's naivety, I will be understood.

## Dharma of Dog Shit

One A.M., the first snowflakes of the storm fog my
glasses, and I walk my Rhodesian Ridgeback mix and
think about the Buddha, whether he ever wandered
behind a canine seeking the perfect spot, whether he
looked away politely as the flea-chewed mutt squatted
along the road or under some meditative tree. The
sage's knotted form bends to scoop because he loves all
beings, and though life is suffering, he would not risk
some transcendent path ruined by a wrong step, his eyes
dark as wells, takes no thought for pride, bends, even
when no one is watching, even when it is the neighbors'
yard defiled, the neighbors (here I'm projecting) with
the *Nuke the Whales* bumper-sticker on their Hummer.
He takes the loving path, saves the gathered waste for
the garden. My dog squats. No one stirs. I scoop, tie off
the bag. Snow crusts on my shoulders, drifts through
my dog's clouding breath. I toss the shit in the trashcan.

## The Missouri by Night

The land slopes its slow way
toward the fog-thick river.
The air's a clamor, rise and fall
of cicadas, tuneless anthem,
drowning the downshifting
trucks, their brakelights blinking
behind trees. Closer, a baseline,
the soft wash of the waves,
trees whispered hymns.
And branches' crack and snap.
The surface, silver pools
in darkness, sways
to some other rhythm.
A chill across my arm. A banshee.
No—coyotes' call and response.

## The Sacrifice Speaks

If I could choose, I would be from a people
with no written language. The climb was hard,
the mountain clogged with scrub-grass
and thorn, the way made no easier
by my load, wood for offering, slung
across my back. They say I did not know,
but even a child can see death in his father's eyes.

Halfway up, I split my palm on a jagged
rock. The dry soil drank the blood. I could hear
it pounding behind my temples. Some other child
might defy his patriarch, his god,
but I let myself be bound, curious to see
whether he cared to stop it. A ram, tangled
in the thicket, my answer: some test passed.
The ram was doubtless unamused.

## Prognosis

The lights buzz. The doctor gives him options.
Now he is a diver, his line cut,
who must rise, contorting,
through the agony of ascension,
and hope to breathe the aching air,
his body forever warped
by the pain of rebirth,
or turn from the flickering surface,
drift forever through the brine-dark depths.

## On Cancer

after Major Jackson

a wasp emerging from its shadowed nest /
swamp reclaiming abandoned towns /  the buzz
of fluorescents on beige walls / a Nature documentary
without a narrator / a man running, his flashlight beam
bobbing against a runoff tunnel / sulfur-steam
rising from an active volcano / the beating
of night wings / a limestone wall exposed
to sea / the skip on the record / the vault breached
and found empty / a ragged timing belt / moths'
bodies in light fixtures / a distant voice, directionless,
rising from cornfield stalks.

## 1492

> . . . because their earlier sojourn in that country
> had been so happy, the Jews regarded the
> expulsion as a terrible betrayal . . .
>
> —Jewish Virtual Library

We found Isaac on the road,
covered in a shroud of flies. Disturbed,
they rose, their angry mass seething
over the thin corpse, entrails spread
by desperate men expecting diamonds.
They got shit.
        As a young man, I asked God
for justice. Now I settle for petty revenge.
I told my people not to look back,
but this banishment was hard, harder
than Lot's, and were it not for His mercy
they would call this the Salt Road
for a thousand years. Perhaps they should.
How long will I wake
believing I smell grapes,
or feel the land's absence,
the candles flickering in the sea breeze?
The people seek comfort, but this is no Exodus,
only another diaspora. Have we sinned
in thinking that place our home?
My fingers are translucent claws

clutching the scroll. There will be no new home for me.
Not since I was a boy have the words felt
so heavy. If this means anything, I cannot see it. Still
I write, bearing witness
for some future I cannot fathom.
Dust settles on my feet, strange, white
like manna, but bitter on the tongue.

# III: Apocalypse

## Report to William Stafford

> . . . tell me if I am right.
> —"Report to Crazy Horse"

You lived long, and carefully.
You knew the prairie wind,
how it can call all through long January nights,
how sometimes settlers would listen
and step from their houses, thin topsoil crunching
under boots or rising to meet bare toes,
and in the morning there would be no trace
of their passing. The storm does this.

I have listened to the wind's song, and I think
I will not live so long. It does not concern me.
But this: I matured in a decade
of madness, assaults on an enemy
we were told was hiding in desert rat holes
or mountain caves, where people hold
centuries-old ways, and older
grudges. (The ones who say this think we are different.
I do not know who they mean by *we*.)
They fight a concept,

a tick growing fat on assassinations, uranium shells,
drone strikes (this is a convenient way of killing
as impersonal as any strip mall).
No one can tell me if they believe they will win,
if they think fighting makes them strong.

You have been gone twenty years now, more than twenty.
They award Peace Prizes to men who have done nothing,
and worse than nothing. The wind does not care
about Mr. Nobel. It does not care about you, Bill,
or me. It is the wind.

I do not know if monsters can be overcome,
if the new great extinction can be halted, or slowed.
I dream of that gleaming face, at times.
Will you tell me what this means?
Yesterday, at dusk, a cold front came battering
against my door, sweeping from the west,
striking bare branches against windows,
stirring the dog as he watched the fire burn low.
A shriek. I rushed in terror to the window.
Two children chased each other in circles, laughing.

## Confessions of a Political Poet

". . . artists who use their media of choice to
advocate specific political agendas should always
warrant our suspicion. . ."

—Sam Lasman

I will confess I have little patience
for pastorals, for experiments, for post-
modern explorations, for poetry written
in circles to subvert patriarchy,

for lyrics that earnestly explore
how communication is impossible.
I confess such things seem a luxury,
and so I embrace unpoeticism,

and admit that I sometimes think
about those bankers who looted millions
from pensions, profiting
on the misery of the soon-to-be

homeless, fantasize about lining up those bastards
and putting two bullets in their heads. I am not
a violent person, I would rather write
about occult patterns which the rain

creates, mixing with oil and garbage
on city streets. How can I write
of the squirrels in my backyard
who antagonize my dog

while Colorado burns, crops wither,
ice caps melt? These are ugly sentiments
for a poet. I can't write small poems
about autumn with Trayvon Martin dead,

and Eric Garner choking on camera,
with "fuck your breath," with Freddie Gray's
spine snapped, with Rekia Boyd's head torn open—
the list outstretches all my poetry.

I can't write about subverting the paradigm of *I*
while the people of Syria are murdered,
while politicians label anyone killed by drones
*enemy combatants*, while polio and T.B. return,

while women die in back-alley
abortions and churches preach *stay
with your abuser*. While football coaches,
Archbishops, politicians cover for rapists,

while the children of the powerful
become the powerful, while wealth
piles in the hands of the rich
and the poor go without jobs, without

healthcare, without hope. I confess
if I knew how, I would rather be a poet
of revolution, to bend my words
against injustice. I confess

I am not that poet—too middle-
class, too white,
too soft-spoken. In my defense,
I can say only this: I

reject the sin of silence.

## Thin Lines

The black man picks up the gun,
flimsy thing, orange-tipped,
as they all have been
since we first learned children's toys
seemed so like men's weapons.
The officer
shoots him dead
in front of the action figures.

> You knew this story's end
> from its first lying line.

The white man marches
down the street—
cars screaming past, drivers caught
for a moment
in terror, even as momentum
carries them past danger.
He strokes an assault rifle.
Later, the police warn him:
*You should have let us know.*

> That is the story
> as local news reported it.

The young man, just out of high school,
flees from a confrontation. Unarmed.
The officer fires.
Bullets split skin.
Perhaps the coroner
will someday say how many.

    The story
    the police tell: a struggle, a flight.

They left the body for hours,
called in riot police,
men made faceless in their armor.
Tire tracks smear flowers across the street.

    The story the neighbors tell: he was due
    to start college on Monday. He was walking
    to his grandmother's.

The neighbors have learned to tell that story first.
Not only what happened,
as described in reports
that pass for truth,
but simpler: the details of a life.
Because the other story metastasizes,
makes every man killed

for selling loose cigarettes
into a criminal,
and criminals into threats,
and threats into bodies.

Even blood does not last.
The stories seep
past their white outlines.

## I Find My Own Name in Shoah Records

> [She] was born in 1896. She was married. Prior
> to WWII she lived in Sarajevo, Yugoslavia.
> During the war she was in Yugoslavia [and] was
> murdered/perished in Lobograd, Camp.
> —Yad Vashem

*I*

Vain, I search for my birth name,
and find the usual pages: student comments,
a book, poems gathering metaphorical dust
in online journals, a scholar who shares my surname

(no relation) and writes on Israeli politics,
a schoolteacher in Brooklyn, a letter I wrote
to the local paper as a child. Nothing
to make one look twice. She is tucked away

among the images,
this woman who shares my name.

No. It must be I share hers.

*II*

What can one say?
I've found only this of her: one page's record,
a survivor attesting to her death. Born in 1896,
in Sarajevo, married, and came to her end
in Lobograd (it appears on no current map).
One scholar says *it did not even have a railway connection.*

This means she died in 1941 or '42,
before they closed that camp,
sent the Jews who were still alive to Auschwitz.
I want to say that, in this small way, she was fortunate.
But what little I find on Lobograd (sometimes, Loborgrad)
speaks of torture, rape.
I cannot imagine, cannot even begin to comprehend,
what it was to pass through those gates,
whether the infamous ones that still today
rise from lips as a curse, or a camp so small
I find it only in footnotes.

*III*

There were other Wassersteins from Sarajevo
who finished in Jasenovac, her male relatives,
one almost certainly her husband. Their lives ended
in a camp that slaughtered more Serbians
than Jews, a place they called monstrous
even by the standards of death camps,
where guards confessed to cutting thousands
of throats in a single night.

A monument stands
at Jasenovac, a flower
or a plume of smoke
opening to the sky.

Lobograd exists only in photos of gates and towers.
An image search shows a yellow-and-white building,
massive, tucked between forest and cornfields,
*lobor grad*: a home for the mentally ill.

*IV*

I am afraid to write this. My mother is German-American,
Protestant. My father converted before they wed.
I have never practiced the faith of his people.
My grandfather, himself a Wasserstein, told me
*I've never been sure I could believe in a god*
*who let that happen.* I never knew him to go to synagogue,
though at his funeral the Rabbi
called him a devout man.

Am I Jew enough to write this poem, to say:
This woman, this stranger, and I
bore the same name,
that once she wed? She was murdered
by fascists forty years before I was born.
Jews tell me I am no Jew. I cannot become a citizen
of Israel (not that I would, that apartheid state).
That would not have saved me. The Jews' matrilineal
reckoning meant nothing to the Nazis.
Jew enough for them.

*V*

Though in Yugoslavia some children
with only one Jewish parent were spared, I'm told.
In this, at least, the Church intervened.

*VI*

The past is erased. That past in particular—
a horror beyond bureaucracy's records,
so much lost even to those who would reconstruct,
who would find and keep the names.

I find no remains of the camp at Lobograd.
Better locations, on the tracks deep into German
forests, were preferred. Now nothing remains,
save the fields, the wide sky.

No. I call it back:
let there be no adjective for that sky.
Let there be no symbol, no signification,
pretending to be adequate to her story,
only this trail of documents: a life, a camp, a death,
an attestation.

## The Golem of Prague

Beside the river was I crafted,
packed and molded of mud, a blind child's
imitation of man. A word
woke me, bound me.

I tell you (my mouth unmoving)
this is no tale of hubris:
my feet of clay have no more of the corpse
than Adam did, before breath
summoned breath. No mad fool stitched me,
nor did the Rabbi wish to be divine.

This I learned: God was alone, so he made man.
The people were alone, so they made me,
breathed life, for a time, that I might
take life in their defense.
Why should they weep that I am
what they dreamed? This is the secret:
the crafter gives a portion of himself. Soon the Rabbi
will return, and wipe one letter clear.

Though I fear the silence, I will answer his call.
The last of my breath will return to him.
And when the last of creation falls,
who will then be made whole?

## Apocalypse Blues

Summer 2012

Sun hammers the clay dry
and burning wind yellows grass.
Fans buzz endlessly, and dogs cease barking.

Fire sweeps from mountains,
explosives rupture sky. Buskers strum
their parched guitars on the corners.

The sandwich board prophets
have fallen away, while radio hums
with *end of days*. Preachers stare silent

at their congregations.
Mourners choke their goodbyes
into the distant, cloudless morning.

A sniper in Syria pops a woman's head
like a heat blister. Bombs in Kandahar,
tear gas in Athens.

Graduates broil in parents' basements,
smoking weed and reading want ads.
The homeless shuffle through deserted streets.

I hear whispers of Mayans and Revelation,
songs of failed love and failed revolution.
The mourning dove does not call for his mate.

Insects crawl into my house to die.
The world tumors and splits . . .

Play her off with minor chords.

## To the Child I Will Never Have

The changes come on so slowly
the pattern emerges only in retrospect.
Droughts become crises,
fires, infernos. No one can name
the tipping point.

The net they've spread under us
is already threadbare, and they plot
openly to cast a new one, wire-thin
and wire-hard, over us. It is finer
than the net that holds us now,
and heavier. I wonder if you will notice.

The diseases we once eradicated
will return for you, along with new ones.
The fascists will return, as they always do,
and your leaders will explain
why the killing of children is necessary.

Learn the names of animals, before they shuffle
down that final path, and the names
of your neighbors. Choose your mate
like you would choose a dog:
be cautious of taking so much,
but, having decided, hold nothing back.

Distrust those who seek profit at the gates
of the temple, and even more those within.
Make something beautiful.

## Albuquerque, Summer

He stopped me on Central,
a man with a face that showed decades
of sun and alcohol, another homeless
Indian. Walk that street any day
and you'll see several. A worn Army
pack carried everything he owned.
Heat clawed from pavement,
enough to make me envy the hawks,
soaring above
the concrete valley.
                    *I won't bullshit you,*
he said. *I just want to buy a beer.*
I'd heard it was cruel to enable.
Those days, I was on poverty
wages, but I slept in a cool apartment,
living on peanut butter and poetry.
I couldn't help him, so I bought him that beer.

## 3 AM, the Plains of San Agustin

There would be no sound if not for the wind,
etching history in dust across the high desert,
pulling sediment laid down by that ancient lake
in whose basin I stand, beneath the arc of stars,
where the first humans to walk this land left tools
beside their ancient path along the water's edge.

Here the land breathes, here the earth finds its edge
along the Great Divide. Here the song is the wind's,
and the rocks became the first tools.
The trick of the place: it was not always desert.
The wheeling sky and the timeless stars
are no more eternal than the land-that-was-lake.

Once the red planet was dotted with lakes,
and once volcanoes, not antennas, cut the edge
of this sky—I am learning to listen to the stars.
I am a guest, interloper of wind,
thin air and slow time of the desert,
which preserves and disdains all our tools.

In this State of pollen-yellow sands, we built tools
to break earth from earth, to flood the sky with lakes
of ash, to shatter millennial quiet of the desert.
In a moment, we carry ourselves to the edge
of annihilation, and trail death on the wind:
this will not disturb the stars.

May I hold in myself the scope of stars,
and in my hands fragile Pleistocene tools,
see the blessings and fury of wind,
for I am here, and here there is a lake,
and the past is with me, and the future's hungry edge,
and I am not the ancient desert,

but I may rest where night meets desert.
May I know the dignity of the stuff of stars,
as the Array whispers *we may be on the edge
of contact*, and *not all tools are tools
of war*. Let me remember the lake,
and the people who drank of it, and the wind.

I stand in desert, amidst monuments to the edge
of our reach, and the stars are not mine, and the lake
is not ours, and our tools are exposed by the wind.

## McCollum and Brown

"No question about it, absolutely they are guilty."
—District Attorney Joe Freeman Britt

Britt tells the jury
*they rammed her panties*
*down her throat.*
*She struggled for five minutes.*
He asks them to hold their breaths
as long as they can,
imagine that desperation,
that doomed clawing for life,
the seconds ticking away
in the eyes of her killers.
For thirty years McCollum and Brown
have felt the weight
of those courtroom seconds.
Thirty years, two teens grown
to middle age as the clock marks
silent minutes. The echo
of locks sliding home, the long-
and-longer wait between meals,
the slow unwinding
of two lives.

The prosecutors had it all along, the cigarette butt,
the DNA that exonerates them—

Britt says it does not; the State disagrees.
He is retired, old, defiant. Can he imagine
so much weight pressing,
the soybeans overhead, the tons of concrete,
glimpses of dark sky, a hand reaching up,
or clasped to a throat . . . how many
days were poised in that moment?
He stands in the courtroom.
*Hold your breath*, he tells the jury.

## You Will Come Up Short

Almost every time.
You will run for 24 hours, run until your calves burn
and your feet are a ruin of blisters,
and reach your destination fifteen seconds late.
The sandbags you stack through the night
will not hold back the floods.
You will look at the rubble of your life.
You will come up short.

The future you work for will always be the future.
The war you rallied against, prayed against,
shouted against, screamed against—
the war you beat your bloody knuckles against
until your arms gave out—
the war will come. The men who started it will grin
over the ashpits of your despair.
You will come up short.

The walls you build around yourself will crack.
The poem you write will fail.
*This* poem will fail.
Your song of protest will not sway the President,
nor the mayor, nor the mayor's dog.
You will pull apart your pockets seeking change,
and finding none, you will give up the milk,
    or the eggs, or the flour.

You will leave the tying run stranded at third base,
and they will laugh and celebrate their triumph
and hope you do not notice they were born there,
on third base, while you fought to take your first swing.

They want you to come up short
because of the color of your skin, or the dirt
caked to your palms, or the shape of your genitals
or the self you need yourself to be,
or whom you love or lust after,
because you do not sound like them,
because you were born elsewhere,
because you were born at all,
because you see their lies,
or because they hate everyone
but themselves, and maybe especially themselves,
and so they cannot stand to see you succeed.

They will leave landmines in your path,
and when they do not know your path,
they will leave landmines everywhere.
They will threaten what you love.
They will promise you a runner-up trophy
if only you stop now. They will take away the trophy
you earned, and if they cannot take it away

they will tell you it was never yours, or never existed,
or that they let you have it.
They will have you thinking since you first crawled
that your legs were theirs,
that your arms were useless to you.
They will cut your tendons.

They will tell you that you are safest if you are silent,
tell you to keep your head low
and your eyes on your folded hands.
They will offer you baubles
and tell you that you can only win
by joining them
and then they will place you in the stands,
far, far up, so you may cheer their triumph with your
bloody mouth,
they will tell you that you can be one of them
if only you put the hammer down,
if only you take up their flag
and their knives
and put them to use.

You will come up short.
They are counting on it.
They have built the world to ensure it.

Almost every time, you will look back and see the long line
of failures and their way will seem appealing, so much easier.
Just put the hammer down,
they will say.

You will see the fear lodged back far behind their eyes,
the pulsing fear, the fear that is a mechanical fist,
always constricting,
and the only way they can loosen it
is to make it grasp you.
And you will know you do not need their fist.

You will come up short.
The blow you strike with all your strength
will not split open the bars.
The alarms will shriek contempt, the hammer will drop
from your hands.
Look at it closely. See the way the grip
was molded for your dirty palm. The edge is chipped
but it is strong. The callouses you have earned
serve you now. Reach down.
The hammer is as heavy as it needs to be.
It was made for you.
Strike again.

## Acoma

The white woman in the visor, heavy turquoise jewelry
hanging over burnt skin, wants to photograph
the cemetery, the only location she's been asked to avoid.

*It is holy to the people of the pueblo*, the guide says.
The husband yellows in his yellow parrot shirt,
asks, *What if our ancestors are buried there?*

Still no, and I'm ashamed for their lack of shame,
for their *tor-till-as*, their loud talk. The group follows
the guide into the church, and I hang back, watching

to see if the woman sneaks a picture. She waddles
inside, huffing in the thin air. Before the People
came to Acoma, they lived on Enchanted Mesa,

drew water and tended crops in the valley,
until a great storm destroyed their access to their home.
Professor Libbey, hearing this, bore the White Man's Burden,

climbed the mesa, pronounced the tale a myth.

The great Princeton man, what did he know
of how quickly the desert wind sweeps humans clear,

whole towns given over to sagebrush,
to cactus, to coyotes. What did he know of a place
whispering of life's fragile ways,
beetles busying themselves

in the wet sand, lizards crouching in abandoned
homes. The land so hostile to man's arrogance
that Libbey forgot himself, never thought

to examine the crevices, the cracks with their birds'
nests, Acoma arrowheads, Acoma pottery,
the mesa offering its truths to the sky.

## The Rate of Universal Expansion is Increasing

It starts with an observation: the universe races away
from us, red-shifted, pulled apart like yarn,
until we're tempted to think ourselves
again the center. The arc
of a rocket splits the sky
and is pulled back. A baseball
freezes for a moment before it descends
to glory or glove. Once we thought
the universe was bound like the Earth,
would reach far and then be
drawn back, but the calculations are precise:
all things fly from each other,
as the surface of an inflating balloon
pulls each point from all the rest.

Gravity will not hold us. There is no mystery
in the end. But birds return
to roost; even updrafts will sustain
the hawk for only so long
before he takes his perch. The stars
spin in their predictable course. For now. For now.

## Prayer

*I*

A comfortable radical, an academic writing careful verse
in a warm office, what would I do
if fascists rose again, slaughterers with perfect death machines?
                                        I cannot say.
There is no answering that day
until it comes,
nor knowing what bells one will strike in warning,
what knotted words of compliance
slip too easily from the tongue.
I have no faith in my bravery, less than in the god revealed
only in silence. Oh, One Who Moves Behind the Facade,
the doors gaping to three-walled houses,
let the illusion-breakers not come for me.
But if they must, grant that I remember Garcia Lorca:
*These fields will be strewn with bodies.*
*I've made up my mind. I'm going to Granada.*

*II*

*Show an affirming flame:*
words renounced,
called back, called back,
as though they had not
echoed through the canyons
before they returned.
      And if my words
become ugly, if I recant
every last kind thought,
if the lines of my face
twist in cruelty,
may these soundings
outlast me.

## Kansas Bible Camp

> Sometime nothing has happened. We are home at the
> beginning of summer . . .
> —William Stafford, "Key of C—Interlude for Marvin"

We scrawled messages on the staff room wall
beneath the kitchen, Eric with his quiet, knowing
smile; Tim, cloaked in labor and silence;
his sister, Tara, who sang like she was cut of fine crystal,
and was all but engaged to James; James, tight-faced, proud
of his ultra-orthodoxy; Mike, with a mind precise
as circuits, always quick to laugh.
We were sixteen, learning what it meant
that we fit in no better at Bible Camp
than at home. Even on the Kansas plains,
we couldn't image horizons big enough
to let us breathe, couldn't imagine anything
on this world to sate us, and so we dreamed
of a New Earth. But still we wrote
in permanent ink.
                    I'm patching my basement wall
and telling you this now. It almost seems
we should have seen what was coming,
as if we only needed some eschatology of our lives.

How Mike would write code for an insurance company
and at night run himself to exhaustion across uneven streets;
how James would drift from church to church
enraged anew at the decadence he always uncovered;
how Tara and I would half-love each other chastely,
how she would meet the girl of her dreams,
then the next, and the next;
how Tim would work twenty hour days
for years, then find himself an architect serving coffee;
how I'd meet Eric in the library parking lot, years later,
a book of children's literature under his arm, and say
*we should get together*, and hear a week after
that he'd sat in his car until the fumes
took him. How I would return to camp,
a decade later, and run my fingers over that wall, our words
long since painted over, replaced
by new generations of teens seeking Jesus,
and how I'm relating this, in the darkness
of my basement, how if I could go back and say
*here is what's coming for us, this is our only kingdom*,
the words would wither on my tongue.

Izzy Wasserstein

## Publication Notes

Grateful acknowledgment is made to these publications, where the following poems first appeared:

*200 New Mexico Poems*: "A Time Traveler Sends a Postcard Home" and "3 AM, the Plains of San Agustin"

*Blood Lotus*: "Touring Topeka, Kansas"

*Coal City Review*: "Kansas Bible Camp."

*Crab Orchard Review*: "Paleontology"

*Heartland!: Poetry of Love, Resistance & Solidarity*: "Report to William Stafford" and "You Will Come Up Short"

*I-70 Review*: "I Rarely Write Before Dawn"

*Innisfree Poetry Journal*: "At the Bend in Cow Creek"

*Pilgrimage*: "Night Shift at the Computer Lab"

*Prairie Schooner*: "Baseball"

*The Rain, Party and Disaster Society*: "85% of Methamphetamine Users Do Not Become Addicts" and "Eureka"

*Red Fez*: "To the Mantis Shrimp"

*Scissors and Spackle*: "The Golem of Prague"

*StarLine*: "Lately I've Been Thinking of Sacrifice"

*The New Verse News*: "Confessions of a Political Poet"

*Wildness House*: "Aubade" and "The Missouri by Night"

# *About the Author*

Izzy Wasserstein was born and raised in Kansas. She teaches English at Washburn University, writes poetry and fiction, and shares a house with a variety of animal companions and the writer Nora E. Derrington. Her work has appeared in *Prairie Schooner*, *Flint Hills Review*, *Crab Orchard Review*, and elsewhere. Her first poetry collection, *This Ecstasy They Call Damnation*, was a 2013 Kansas Notable book. She likes to slowly run long distances. Her website is izzywasserstein.com.

# Acknowledgments

My thanks go out to all those who made this book possible. Many of these poems received valuable feedback from members of my writers' group, including Ande Davis, C. Malcolm Ellsworth, Miranda Ericsson, Sandy Morgan, Loretta F. Ross, Leah Sewell, Melissa Sewell, and Timothy Volpert.

I also received amazing feedback and support from Lisa D. Chávez, Marisa P. Clark, Lisa Hase-Jackson, Gary Jackson, and Juan J. Morales.

The 2017 class of Clarion West provided me friendship, insight, and space to be myself when I desperately needed all three. Thanks, Team Eclipse.

My parents' love, wisdom, and support have done much to make this book possible, from instilling in me a love of reading to always encouraging me as I pursued my tangled path.

And most of all, to my brilliant, kind, and wise partner and spouse Nora E. Derrington, my first and best reader and my favorite person. It is no exaggeration to say this book would not exist without you, Liz.

# WWW.MEADOWLARK-BOOKS.COM

Specializing in Books by Authors from the Heartland since 2014

GREEN BIKE

Read

A Meadowlark Book

meadowlark-books.com

MoonStain
poetry by Ronda Miller

Water Signs
Poems by
Ronda Miller

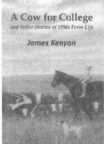

A Cow for College
and Other Stories of 1950s Farm Life

James Kenyon

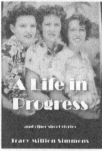

A Life in Progress
and other short stories
Tracy Million Simmons

To Leave
a Shadow

Michael D. Graves

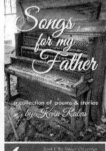

Songs
for my
Father
a collection of poems & stories
by Kevin Rabas

Walking on Water
poems by
Cheryl Unruh

Shadow
of Death

Michael D. Graves

What Lies Beyond

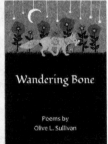

Wandering Bone

Poems by
Olive L. Sullivan

Everyday Magic
Field Notes on the
Mundane and the Miraculous

Caryn Mirriam-Goldberg

DRIVING TOGETHER

86473244R00066

Made in the USA
San Bernardino, CA
28 August 2018